P9-BIK-945

THE RIGHT TO USEFUL
UNEMPLOYMENT

By the same author

Ivan Illich

THE RIGHT TO USEFUL

UNEMPLOYMENT

and its professional enemies

MARION BOYARS · LONDON · BOSTON

First published in Great Britain in 1978
by Marion Boyars Publishers Ltd
18 Brewer Street, London W1R 4AS

Reprinted 1978

Published in Canada by Burns & MacEachern Ltd.,
Suite 3, 62 Railside Road, Don Mills, Ontario M3A 1A6

Australian distribution by Thomas C. Lothian Pty Ltd
4-12 Tattersalls Lane
Melbourne, Victoria 3000

© Ivan Illich 1978

ALL RIGHTS RESERVED

ISBN 0 7145 2628 2 Cased edition
ISBN 0 7145 2663 0 Paper edition

Any paperback edition of this book whether published
simultaneously with, or subsequent to, the cased edition is sold
subject to the condition that it shall not, by way of trade, be lent,
resold, hired out, or otherwise disposed of, without the publisher's
consent, in any form of binding or cover other than that in which
it was published.

No part of this publication may be reproduced,
stored in a retrieval system, or transmitted, in any form or by any
means, electronic, mechanical, photocopying, recording or otherwise, except brief extracts for the purposes of review, without
the prior written permission of the copyright owner and publisher

Printed and bound in Great Britain by
REDWOOD BURN LIMITED
Trowbridge & Esher

CONTENTS

ABOUT THE AUTHOR

Ivan Illich was born in 1926. He studied theology and philosophy at the Gregorian University in Rome and obtained a doctorate in history at the University of Salzburg. He went to the United States in 1951, where he served as assistant pastor in an Irish-Puerto Rican parish in New York City. From 1956 to 1960 he was vice-rector of the Catholic University of Puerto Rico. Illich was a co-founder of the Center for Intercultural Documentation (CIDOC), in Cuernavaca, Mexico, where he directed research seminars on 'Institutional Alternatives in a Technological Society', with special focus on Latin America until 1976. Ivan Illich's writings have appeared in many newspapers and journals including *The New York Times, The New York Review of Books, The Saturday Review, Esprit, Kursbuch, Siempre, Excelsior de Mexico, America, Commonweal, Les Temps Modernes, Le Monde, Le Nouvel Observateur, The Ecologist, The Guardian* and *The Lancet*. He is the author of *Celebration of Awareness, Deschooling Society, Tools for Conviviality, Energy and Equity, Limits to Medicine: Medical Nemesis – the Expropriation of Health*, and (with others) *Disabling Professions*.

FOREWORD

In the last decade or so I have prepared and published a number of essays* on the industrial mode of production. During this period, I have focused on the processes through which growing dependence on mass-produced goods and services gradually erodes

*Deschooling Society (Calder & Boyars, 1971)
Tools for Conviviality (Calder & Boyars, 1973)
Energy & Equity (Calder & Boyars, 1974)
Limits to Medicine: Medical Nemesis – The Expropriation of Health (Marion Boyars, 1976)
Disabling Professions (Marion Boyars, 1977)

7

the conditions necessary for a convivial life. Examining distinct areas of economic growth, each essay demonstrates a general rule: use-values are inevitably destroyed when the industrial mode of production achieves the predominance that I have termed 'radical monopoly'. This and my previous essays describe how industrial growth produces the modernization of poverty.

Modernized poverty appears when the intensity of market dependence reaches a certain threshold. Subjectively, it is the experience of frustrating affluence that occurs in persons mutilated by their reliance on the riches of industrial productivity. It deprives those affected by it of their freedom and power to act autonomously, to live creatively; it confines them to survival through being plugged into market relations. And precisely because this new impotence is so deeply experienced, it is with difficulty expressed. For example, we are the witnesses of a barely perceptible transformation in ordinary language: verbs which formerly expressed satisfying actions have been replaced by nouns which name packages designed for passive consumption only – 'to learn' becomes 'to accumulate credits'. A profound change in individual and social self-images is here reflected. And the layman is not the only one who has difficulty in accurately expressing what he experiences. The professional economist is unable to recognize the poverty that his conventional instruments fail to uncover. Nevertheless, the new mutant of impoverishment continues to spread. The peculiarly modern

8

inability to use personal endowments, community wealth, and environmental resources in an autonomous way infects every aspect of life where a professionally engineered commodity has succeeded in replacing a culturally shaped use-value. The opportunity to experience personal and social satisfaction outside the market is thus destroyed. I am poor, for example, when the use-value of my feet is lost because I live in Los Angeles or work on the thirty-fifth floor of a sky-scraper.

This new impotence-producing poverty must not be confused with the widening gap between the consumption of rich and poor in a world where basic needs are increasingly shaped by industrial commodities. This gap is the form traditional poverty assumes in an industrial society, and the conventional terms of class struggle appropriately reveal and reduce it. I further distinguish modernized poverty from the burdensome price exacted by the externalities which increased levels of production spew into the environment. It is clear that these kinds of pollution, stress, and taxation are unequally imposed. Correspondingly, defences against such depredations are unequally distributed. But like the new gaps in access, such inequities in social costs are aspects of industrialized poverty for which economic indicators and objective verification can be found. Such is not true for the industrialized impotence that affects both rich and poor. Where this kind of poverty reigns, life without addictive access to commodities is rendered impossible or criminal – or both. Making do without consumption becomes impossible, not just for the average consumer, but even for the poor. All forms of welfare, from affirmitive action to job training, are of no help. The liberty to design and craft one's own distinctive dwelling is abolished in favour of the bureaucratic provision of standardized housing in the United States, Cuba or Sweden. The organization of employment, skills, building resources, of rules and credit favour shelter as a commodity rather than as an activity. Whether the product is provided by an entrepreneur or an apparatchik, the effective result is the same: citizen impotence, our specifically modern experience of poverty.

Wherever the shadow of economic growth touches us, we are left useless unless employed on a job or engaged in consumption: the attempt to build a house or set a bone outside the control of certified specialists appears as anarchic conceit. We lose sight of our resources, lose control over the environmental conditions which make these resources applicable, lose taste for self-reliant coping with challenges from without and anxiety from within. Take childbirth in Mexico today. Delivery without professional care has become unthinkable for those women whose husbands hold regular employment and, therefore, access to social services, no matter how marginal or tenuous, is denied. They move in circles where the production of babies faithfully reflects the patterns of industrial outputs. Yet their sisters who live in the slums of the poor or the villages of the isolated still feel quite competent to give birth on their own mats; they are still unaware that they face à modern indictment of criminal neglect toward their child. But as professionally engineered delivery models reach these independent women, the desire, competence, and conditions for autononmous behaviour are being destroyed.

For advanced industrial society, the modernization of poverty means that people are helpless to recognize evidence unless it has been certified by a professional – be he a television weather commentator or an educator; organic discomfort becomes intolerably threatening unless it has been medicalized into dependence on a therapist; neighbours and friends are lost unless vehicles bridge the separating distance (created by the vehicles in the first place). In short, most of the time we find ourselves out of touch with our world, out of sight of those for whom we work, out of tune with what we feel.

This essay is a postscript to my book, *Tools for Conviviality*, published in 1973. It reflects the changes which have occurred during the past decade, both in economic reality and in my own perceptions of it. It assumes a rather large increase in the non-technical, ritual, and symbolic powers of our major technological and bureaucratic systems, and a corresponding decrease in their scientific, technical, and instrumental credibility. In 1968, for example, it was still quite easy to dismiss organized lay resistance to professional dominance as nothing more than a throwback to romantic, obscurantist or élitist fantasies. The grass roots, common sense assessment of technological systems which I then outlined, seemed childish or retrograde to the political leaders of citizen activism, and to the 'radical' professionals who laid claim to the tutorship of the poor by means of their special knowledge. The reorganization of late industrial society around professionally defined needs, problems, and solutions was still the commonly accepted value implicit in ideological, political, and juridical systems otherwise clearly and sometimes violently opposed to one another.

Now the picture has changed. A hallmark of advanced and enlightened technical competence is a self-confident community, neighbourhood or group of citizens engaged in the systematic analysis and consequent ridicule of the 'needs', 'problems', and 'solutions' defined for them by the agents of professional establishments. In the sixties, lay opposition to legislation based on expert opinion still sounded like antiscientific bigotry. Today, lay confidence in public policies based upon the expert's opinion is tenuous indeed. Now thousands reach their own judgments and, at great cost, engage in citzien action without any professional tutorship; through personal, independent effort, they gain the scientific information they need. Sometimes risking limb, freedom, and respectability, they bear witness to a newly mature scientific attitude. They know, for example, that the quality and amount of technical evidence sufficiently conclusive to oppose atomic power plants, the multiplication of intensive care units, compulsory education, foetal monitoring, psycho-surgery, electro-shock treatment, or genetic engineering is also simple and clear enough for the layman to grasp and utilize.

Ten years ago, compulsory schooling was still protected by powerful taboos. Today, its defenders are almost exclusively either teachers whose jobs depend upon it or Marxist ideologues who defend professional knowledge-holders in a shadow battle against the hip-bourgeoisie. Ten years ago, the myths about the effectiveness of modern medical institutions were still unquestioned. For example, most textbooks accepted the beliefs that adult life expectancy was increasing, that treatment for cancer postponed death, that the availability of doctors produced greater infant survival rates. Since then people have 'discovered' what vital statistics have always shown – adult life expectancy has not changed in any socially significant way over the last few generations, is lower in most rich countries today than in our grand-parents' time, and lower than in many poor nations. Ten years ago, universal access to post-secondary schooling, to adult education, to preventative medicine, to highways, to a wired global village were still prestigious goals. Today, the great myth-making rituals organized around education, transportation, health care, urbanization have indeed been partly demystified; they have however not yet been dis-established.

Shadow prices and increased consumption gaps are important aspects of the new poverty. But my principal interest is directed towards a different concomitant of modernization – the process through which autonomy is undermined, satisfaction is dulled, experience is flattened out, needs are frustrated for nearly everyone. For example, I have examined the society-wide obstacles to mutual presence which are necessary side effects of energy-intensive transportation. I have wanted to define the power limits of motors equitably used to increase access to one another. I recognize, of course, that high speeds inevitably impose a skewed distribution of harriedness, noise, pollution, and enjoyment of privilege. But my emphasis is other. My arguments are focused on the negative *internalities* of modernity – such as time-consuming acceleration, sick-making health care, stupefying education. The unequal distribution of these ersatz benefits, or the unequal imposition of their negative *externalities*, are corollaries to my basic argument. I am interested in the direct and specific effects of modernized poverty, in human tolerance for such effects and in the possibility of escaping the new misery. I share with others a deep desire to see greater justice. I am absolutely opposed to the unjust distribution of what can be genuinely shared with pleasure. But I have found it necessary, these last few years, to examine carefully the objects of any and every redistribution proposal. Today I see my task even more clearly than when I first started talking and writing about the counterproductive mythmaking that is latent in all late industrial enterprises. My aim has been to detect and denounce the false affluence which is *always* unjust because it can only frustrate. Through this kind of analysis one can begin to develop the theory which would inspire the social regeneration

14

possible for twentieth-century man.

During these last years I have found it necessary to examine, again and again, the correlation between the nature of tools and the meaning of justice that prevails in the society that uses them. I could not help but observe the decline of freedom in societies in which rights are shaped by expertise. I had to weigh the trade-offs between new tools that enhance the production of commodities and those equally modern ones that permit the generation of values in use; between rights to mass-produced commodities and the level of liberties that permit satisfying and creative personal expression; between paid employment and useful unemployment. And in each dimension of the trade-off between heteronomous management and autonomous action I found that the language that would permit us to insist on the latter has to be recovered with pains. I am, of course, like those whom I seek as my readers, so clearly committed to a radically equitable distribution of goods, rights and jobs that I find it almost unnecessary to insist on our struggle for this side of justice. I find it much more important and difficult to deal with its complement: the Politics of Conviviality. I use this term in the technical sense that I have given to it in *Tools for Conviviality*. There the term designates the struggle for an equitable distribution of the liberty to generate use-values and for the instrumentation of this liberty by the assignment of an absolute priority to the production of those industrial and professional com-modities that confer on the least advantaged the greatest power to generate values in use.

Convivial Politics are based on the insight that in a modern society both wealth and jobs can be equitably shared and enjoyed in liberty only when both are limited by a political process. Excessive forms of wealth and prolonged formal employment, no matter how well distributed, destroy the social, cultural, and environmental conditions for equal productive freedom. *Bits* and *watts* (which stand for units of information and of energy respectively) when packaged into any mass-produced commodity in amounts that pass a threshold, *inevitably* constitute impoverishing wealth. Such impoverishing wealth is either too rare to be shared, or it is destructive of the freedom and liberty of the weakest. With each of my essays I have attempted to make a contribution to the political process by which the socially critical thresholds of enrichment are recognized by citizens and translated into society-wide ceilings or limits.

INTRODUCTION

Fifty years ago, most of the words heard by an American were personally spoken to him as an individual, or to somebody standing nearby. Only occasionally did words reach him as the undifferentiated member of a crowd – in the classroom or church, at a rally or a circus. Words were mostly like handwritten, sealed letters, and not like the junk that now pollutes our mail. Today, words that are directed to one person's attention have become rare. Engineered staples of images, ideas, feelings and opinions, packaged and delivered through the media, assault our sensibilities with round-the-clock regularity. Two points now become evident: 1) what is occurring with language fits the pattern of an increasingly wide range of need-satisfaction relationships; 2) this replacement of convivial means by manipulative industrial ware is truly universal, and is relentlessly making the New York teacher, the Chinese commune member, the Bantu schoolboy, and the Brazilian sergeant alike. In this postscript to my essay *Tools for Conviviality* I shall do three things: 1) describe the character of a commodity/market-intensive society in which the very abundance of commodities paralyzes the autonomous creation of use-values; 2) insist on the hidden role that professions play in such a society by shaping its needs; 3) expose some illusions and propose some strategies to break the professional power that perpetuates market dependence.

[1]

DISABLING MARKET INTENSITY

Crisis has come to mean that moment when doctors, diplomats, bankers and assorted social engineers take over and liberties are suspended. Like patients, nations go on the critical list. *Crisis*, the Greek term that has designated 'choice' or 'turning point' in all modern languages now means 'driver, step on the gas'. Crisis now evokes an ominous but tractable threat against which money, manpower and management can be rallied. Intensive care for the dying, bureaucratic tutelage for the victim of discrimination, fission for the energy glutton, are typical responses.

Crisis, understood in this way, is always good for executives and commissars, especially those scavengers who live on the side effects of yesterday's growth: educators who live on society's alienation, doctors who prosper on the work and leisure that have destroyed health, politicians who thrive on the distribution of welfare which, in the first instance, was financed by those assisted. Crisis understood as a call for acceleration not only puts more power under the control of the driver, while squeezing the passengers more tightly into their safety belts; it also justifies the depredation of space, time and resources for the sake of motorized wheels and it does so to the detriment of people who want to use their feet.

But crisis need not have this meaning. It need not imply a headlong rush for the escalation of management. Instead, it can mean the instant of choice, that marvellous moment when people suddenly become aware of their self-imposed cages, and of the possibility of a different life. And *this* is the crisis, that, as a choice, confronts both the United States and the world today.

A world-wide choice

In only a few decades, the world has become an amalgam. Human responses to everyday occurrences have been standardized. Though languages and gods still appear to be different, people daily join the stupendous majority who march to the beat of the very same mega-machine. The light switch by the door has replaced the dozens of ways in which fires, candles and lanterns were formerly kindled. In ten years, the number of switch-users in the world has tripled: flush and paper have become essential conditions for the relief of the bowels. Light that does not flow from high-voltage networks and hygiene without tissue paper spell poverty for ever more people. Expectations grow, while hopeful trust in one's own competence and the concern for others rapidly decline.

The now soporific, now raucous intrusion of the media reaches deeply into the commune, the village, the corporation, the school. The sounds made by the editors and announcers of programmed texts daily pervert the words of a spoken language into the building blocks for packaged messages. Today, one must either be isolated and cut off, or a carefully guarded, affluent drop-out, to allow one's children to play in an environment where they listen to people rather than to stars, speakers, or instructors. All over the world, one can see the rapid encroachment of the disciplined acquiescence that characterizes the audience, the client, the customer. The standardization of human action grows apace.

It now becomes clear that most of the world's communities are facing exactly the same critical issue: people must either remain ciphers in the conditioned crowd that surges towards greater dependence (thus necessitating savage battles for a share of the drugs to feed their habit), or they must find the courage that alone saves in a panic: to stand still and look around for another way out than the obvious marked exit.

21

But many, when told that Bolivians, Canadians and Hungarians all face the same fundamental choice, are not simply annoyed, but deeply offended. The idea appears not only foolish but shocking. They fail to detect the sameness in the new bitter degradation that underlies the hunger of the Indian in the Altiplano, the neurosis of the worker in Amsterdam, and the cynical corruption of the bureaucrat in Warsaw.

Towards a culture for staples

Development has had the same effect in all societies: everyone has been enmeshed in a new web of dependence on commodities that flow out of the same kind of machines, factories, clinics, television studios, think tanks. To satisfy this dependence, more of the same must be produced: standardized, engineered goods, designed for the future consumers who will be trained by the engineer's agent to need what he or she is offered. These products – be they tangible goods or intangible services – constitute the industrial staple. Their imputed monetary value as a commodity is determined by state and market in varying proportions. Thus different cultures become insipid residues of traditional styles of action, washed up in one world-wide wasteland: an arid terrain devastated by the machinery needed to produce and consume. On the banks of the Seine and those of the Niger, people have unlearned how to milk, because the white stuff now comes from the grocer. (Thanks to more richly endowed consumer protection, it is less poisonous in France than in Mali.) True, more babies get cow's

22

milk, but the breasts of both rich and poor dry up. The addicted consumer is born when the baby cries for the bottle: when the organism is trained to reach for milk from the grocer and to turn away from the breast that thus defaults. Autonomous and creative human action, required to make man's universe bloom, atrophies. Roofs of shingle or thatch, tile or slate, are displaced by concrete for the few and corrugated plastic for the many. Neither jungle marshes nor ideological biases have prevented the poor and the socialist from rushing onto the highways of the rich, the roads leading them into the world where economists replace priests. The mint stamps out all local treasures and idols. Money devalues what it cannot measure. The crisis, then, is the same for all: the choice of more or less dependence upon industrial commodities. *More* dependence means the rapid and complete destruction of cultures which determine the criteria for satisfying subsistence activities. *Less* means the variegated flowering of use-values in modern cultures of intense activity. Although hard to imagine for those already accustomed to living inside the supermarket, a structure different only in name from a ward for idiots, the choice is essentially the same for both rich and poor.

Present-day industrial society organizes life around commodities. Our market-intensive societies measure material progress by the increase in the volume and variety of commodities produced. And taking our cue from this sector, we measure social progress by the distribution of access to these commodities.

23

Economics has been developed as propaganda for the takeover by large-scale commodity producers. Socialism has been debased to a struggle against handicapped distribution, and welfare economics has identified the public good with opulence – the humiliating opulence of the poor in the schools, hospitals, jails and asylums of the United States and other western countries.

By disregarding all trade-offs to which no price tag is attached, industrial society has created an urban landscape that is unfit for people unless they devour each day their own weight in metals and fuels, a world in which the constant need for protection against the unwanted results of more things and more commands has generated new depths of discrimination, impotence and frustration. The establishment-orientated ecological movement so far has further strengthened this trend: it has concentrated attention on faulty industrial technology, and, at best, on exploitation of industrial production by private owners. It has questioned the depletion of natural resources, the inconvenience of pollution, and net transfers of power. But even when price tags are attached to reflect the environmental impact, the disvalue of nuisance, or the cost of polarization, we still do not see clearly that the division of labour, the multiplication of commodities and dependence on them have forcibly substituted standardized packages for almost everything people formerly did or made on their own.

For two decades now, about fifty languages have died each year; half of all those still spoken in 1950

24

survive only as subjects for doctoral theses. And what distinct languages do remain to witness the incomparably different ways of seeing, using, and enjoying the world, now sound more and more alike. Consciousness is colonized everywhere by imported labels. Yet, even those who do worry about the loss of cultural and genetic variety, or about the multiplication of long-impact isotopes, do not advert to the irreversible depletion of skills, stories, and senses of form. And this progressive substitution of industrial goods and services for useful but non-marketable values has been the shared goal of political factions and regimes otherwise violently opposed to one another.

In this way, ever larger pieces of our lives are so transformed that life itself comes to depend almost exclusively on the consumption of commodities sold on the world market. The United States corrupts its farmers to provide grain to a regime which increasingly stakes its legitimacy on the ability to deliver ever more grain. Of course, the two regimes allocate resources by different methods: here, by the wisdom of pricing; there, by the wisdom of planners. But the political opposition between proponents of alternate methods of allocation only masks the similar ruthless disregard of personal dignity and freedom by all factions and parties.

Energy policy is a good example for the profound identity in the world-views of the self-styled socialist and the so-called capitalist supporters of the industrial system. Possibly excluding such places as Cambodia, about which I am uninformed, no governing élite nor any socialist opposition can conceive of a desirable future that would be based on per capita energy consumption of a magnitude inferior to that which now prevails in Europe. All existing political parties stress the need for energy-intensive production – albeit with Chinese discipline – while failing to comprehend that the corresponding society will further deny people the free use of their limbs. Here sedans and there buses push bicycles off the road. All governments stress an employment-intensive force of production, but are unwilling to recognize that jobs can also destroy the use-value of free time. They all stress a more objective and complete professional definition of people's needs, but are insensitive to the consequent expropriation of life.

In the late Middle Ages the stupefying simplicity of the heliocentric model was used as an argument to discredit the new astronomy. Its elegance was interpreted as naivete. In our days, use-value centred theories that analyze the social costs generated by established economics are certainly not rare. Such theories are being proposed by dozens of outsiders, who often identify them with radical technology, ecology, community life-styles, smallness, or beauty. As an excuse to avoid looking at these theories, the frequent failure of their proponents' experiments in personal living are held against them and magnified. Just as the legendary inquisitor refused to look through Galileo's telescope, so most modern economists refuse to look at an analysis that might displace the conventional centre of their economic system. The new analytical systems would force us to recognize the obvious: that the generation of non-marketable use-values must inevitably occupy the centre of any culture that provides a programme for satisfactory life to a majority of its members. Cultures are programmes for activities, not for firms. Industrial society destroys this centre by polluting it with the measured output of corporations, public or private, degrading what people do or make on their own. As a consequence, societies have been transformed into huge zero-sum games, monolithic delivery systems in which every gain for one turns into a loss or burden for another, while true satisfaction is denied to both.

On the way, innumerable sets of infrastructures in which people coped, played, ate, made friends, and loved have been destroyed. A couple of so-called development decades have sufficed to dismantle traditional patterns of culture from Manchuria to Montenegro. Prior to these years, such patterns permitted people to satisfy most of their needs in a subsistence mode. After these years, plastic had replaced pottery, carbonated beverages replaced water, Valium replaced camomile tea, and records replaced guitars. All through history, the best measure for bad times was the percentage of food eaten that had to be purchased. In good times, most families got most of their nutrition from what they grew or acquired in a network of gift relationships. Until late in the eighteenth century, more than 99 per cent of the world's food was produced inside the horizon that the consumer could see from the church steeple or minaret. Laws that tried to control the number of chickens and pigs within the city walls suggest that, except for a few large urban areas, more than half of all food eaten was also cultivated within the city. Before World War II, less than 4 per cent of all food eaten was transported into the region from abroad, and these imports were largely confined to the eleven cities which then contained more than two million inhabitants. Today, 40 per cent of all people survive only because they have access to inter-regional markets. A future in which the world market of capital and goods would be severely reduced is as much a taboo today as a modern world in which active people would use modern convivial tools to create an abundance of use-values that liberated them from consumption. One can see in this pattern a reflection of the belief that useful activities by which people both express and satisfy their needs can be replaced indefinitely by standardized goods or services.

The modernization of poverty

Beyond a certain threshold, the multiplication of commodities induces impotence, the incapacity to grow food, to sing, or to build. The toil and pleasure of the human condition become a faddish privilege restricted to some of the rich. When Kennedy launched the Alliance for Progress, Acatzingo, like most Mexican villages of its size, had four groups of musicians who played for a drink and served the population of eight hundred. Today, records and radios, hooked up to loudspeakers, drown out local talent. Occasionally, in an act of nostalgia, a collection is taken up to bring a band of drop-outs from the university for some special holiday to sing the old songs. On the day Venezuela legislated the right of each citizen to 'housing', conceived of as a commodity, three-quarters of all families found that their self-built dwellings were thereby degraded to the status of hovels. Furthermore – and this is the rub – self-building was now prejudiced. No house could be legally started without the submission of an approved architect's plan. The useful refuse and junk of Caracas, up until then re-employed as excellent building materials, now created a problem of solid-waste disposal. The man who produces his own 'housing' is looked down upon as a deviant who refuses to cooperate with the local pressure group for the delivery of mass-produced housing units. Also, innumerable regulations have appeared which brand his ingenuity as illegal, or even criminal. This example illustrates how the poor are the first to suffer when a new kind of commodity castrates one of the traditional subsistence crafts. The *useful unemployment* of the jobless poor is sacrificed to the expansion of the labour market. 'Housing' as a self-chosen activity, just like any other freedom for useful unemployment of time off the job, becomes the privilege of some deviant, often the idle rich.

An addiction to paralyzing affluence, once it becomes engrained in a culture, generates 'modernized poverty'. This is a form of disvalue necessarily associated with the proliferation of commodities. This

rising disutility of industrial mass products has es-
caped the attention of economists, because it is not
accessible to their measurements, and of social servicers, because it cannot be 'operationalized'. Economists have no effective means of including in their
calculations the society-wide loss of a kind of satisfaction that has no market equivalent. Thus, one could
today define economists as the members of a fraterni-
ty which only accepts people who, in the pursuit of
their professional work, can practice a trained social
blindness towards the most fundamental trade-off in
contemporary systems, both East and West: the
decline in the individual-personal ability to do or to
make, which is the price of every additional degree of
commodity affluence.

The existence and nature of modernized poverty
remained hidden, even in ordinary conversation, as
long as it primarily affected the poor. As development, or modernization, reached the poor – those who
until then had been able to survive in spite of being
excluded from the market economy – they were
systematically compelled to survive through buying into
a purchasing system which, for them, always and
necessarily meant getting the dregs of the market.
Indians in Oaxaca who formerly had no access to
schools are now drafted into school to 'earn' certificates
that measure precisely their inferiority relative to the
urban population. Furthermore – and this is again the
rub – without this piece of paper they can no longer
enter even the building trades. Modernization of 'needs'
always adds new discrimination to poverty.

Modernized poverty has now become the common experience of all except those who are so rich that they can drop out in luxury. As one facet of life after another becomes dependent on engineered supplies, few of us escape the recurrent experience of impotence. The average United States consumer is bombarded by a hundred advertisements per day, and reacts to many of them – more often than not – in a negative way. Even well-heeled shoppers acquire, with each new commodity, a fresh experience of disutility. They suspect they have purchased something of doubtful value, perhaps soon useless, or even dangerous, and something that calls for an array of even more expensive complements. Affluent shoppers organize: they usually begin with demands for quality control, and not infrequently generate consumer resistance. Across the tracks, slum neighbourhoods 'unplug' themselves from service and 'care', from social work in South Chicago and from textbooks in Kentucky. Rich and poor are almost ready to recognize clearly a new form of frustrating wealth in the further expansions of a market-intensive culture. Also, the affluent come to sense their own plight as it is mirrored in the poor, though for the moment this intimation has not developed beyond a kind of romanticism.

The ideology that identifies progress with affluence is not restricted to the rich countries. The same ideology degrades non-marketable activities even in areas where, until recently, most needs were still met through a subsistence mode of life. For example, under Mao the Chinese – drawing inspiration from their own tradition – seemed willing and able to redefine technical progress and to opt for the bicycle over the jet plane. They stressed local self-determination as a goal of inventive people, rather than as a means for national defence. But by 1977, their propaganda was glorying in China's industrial capacity to deliver more health care, education, housing, and general welfare – at a lower cost. Merely tactical functions are provisionally assigned to the herbs in the bag of the barefoot doctor and to labour-intensive production methods. Here, as in other areas of the world, heteronomous – that is, other-directed – production of goods, standardized for categories of anonymous consumers, fosters unrealistic and ultimately frustrating expectations. Furthermore, the process inevitably corrupts the trust of people in their own and their neighbours' ever-surprising autonomous competences. China simply represents the latest example of the particular western version of modernization through intensive market dependence seizing a traditional society as no cargo cult did at its most irrational extreme.

The history of needs

In both traditional and modern societies, an important change has occurred in a very short period: the means for satisfaction of needs have been radically altered. The motor has sapped the muscle; instruction has deadened self-confident curiosity. As a consequence, both needs and wants have acquired a character for which there is no historical precedent. For the first time, needs have become almost exclusively coterminous with commodities. As long as most people walked wherever they wanted to go, they felt restrained mainly when their *freedom* was restricted. Now that they depend on transportation in order to move, they claim not a freedom but a *right* to passenger miles. And as ever more vehicles provide ever more people with such 'rights', the freedom to walk is degraded and eclipsed by the provision of these rights. For most people, wants follow suit. They cannot even imagine liberation from universal passengerhood, that is the liberty of modern man in a modern world to move on his own.

This situation, by now a rigid interdependence of needs and market, is legitimated through appeal to the expertise of an élite whose knowledge, by its very nature, cannot be shared. Economists of rightist as well as leftist persuasion vouch to the public that an increase in jobs depends on more energy; educators persuade the public that law, order, and productivity depend on more instruction; gynaecologists claim that the quality of infant life depends on their involvement in childbirth. Therefore, the near-universal extension of market intensity in the world's economies cannot be effectively questioned as long as the immunity of the élites which legitimize the nexus between commodity and satisfaction has not been destroyed. The point is well illustrated by a woman who told me about the birth of her third child. Having borne two children, she felt both competent and experienced. She was in hospital and sensed the child coming. She called the nurse, who, instead of helping, rushed for a sterile towel to press the baby's head back into the womb and ordered the mother to stop pushing because, 'Dr. Levy has not yet arrived'.

But this is the moment for public decision, for political action instead of professional management. Modern societies, rich or poor, can move in either of two opposite directions: they can produce a new bill of goods — albeit safer, less wasteful, more easily shared — and thereby further intensify their dependence on consumer staples. Or, they can take a totally new approach to the inter-relationship between needs and satisfactions. In other words, societies can either retain their market-intensive economies, changing only the design of the output, or they can reduce their dependence on commodities. The latter entails the adventure of imagining and constructing new frameworks in which individuals and communities can develop a new kind of modern toolkit. This would be organized so as to permit people to shape and satisfy an expanding proportion of their needs directly and personally.

The first direction represents a continuing identification of technical progress with the multiplication of commodities. The bureaucratic managers of egalitarian persuasion and the technocrats of welfare would converge in a call for austerity: to shift from goods, such as jets, that obviously cannot be shared, to so-called 'social' equipment, like buses; to distribute more equitably the decreasing hours of employment available and ruthlessly limit the typical work week to about twenty hours on the job; to draft the new resource of unemployed life-time into retraining or voluntary service on the model of Mao, Castro, or Kennedy. This new stage of industrial society – though socialist, effective, and rational – would simply usher in a new state of the culture that downgraded the satisfaction of wants into repetitive relief of imputed needs through engineered staples. At its best, this alternative would produce goods and services in smaller quantities, distribute them more equitably, and foster less envy. The symbolic participation of people in deciding what ought to be made might be transferred from a buck in the market to a gawk in the political assembly. The environmental impact of production could be softened. Among commodities, services, especially the various forms of social control, would certainly grow much faster than the manufacture of goods. Huge sums are already being spent on the oracle industry so that government prophets can spew out 'alternative' scenarios designed to shore up this first choice. Interestingly, many of them have already reached the conclusion that the cost of the social controls necessary to enforce austerity in an ecologically feasible, but still industry-centred society would be intolerable.

The second choice would bring down the curtain on absolute market dominance, and foster an ethic of austerity for the sake of widespread satisfying action. If in the first alternative austerity would mean the individual's acceptance of managerial ukazes for the

35

sake of increased institutional productivity, austerity in the second alternative would mean that social virtue by which people recognize and decide limits on the maximum amount of instrumented power that anyone may claim, both for his own satisfaction and in the service of others. This convivial austerity inspires a society to protect personal use-value against disabling enrichment. Under such protection against disabling affluence many distinct cultures would arise, each modern and each emphasizing the dispersed use of modern tools. Convivial austerity so limits the use of any tool that tool ownership would lose much of its present power. If bicycles are owned here by the commune, there by the rider, nothing is changed about the essentially convivial nature of the bicycle as a tool. Such commodities would still be produced in large measure by industrial methods, but they would be seen and evaluated differently. Now, commodities are viewed mostly as staples that directly feed the needs shaped by their designers. In the second option, they would be valued either as raw materials or as tools that permitted people to generate use-values in maintaining the subsistence of their respective communities. But this choice depends, of course, on a Copernican revolution in our perception of values. At present, we see consumer goods and professional services at the centre of our economic system, and specialists relate our needs exclusively to this centre. In contrast, the social inversion contemplated here would assign use-values created and personally valued by people themselves to the centre.

It is true that people have recently lost the confidence to shape their own desires. The world-wide discrimination against the autodidact has vitiated many people's confidence in determining their own goals and needs. But the same discrimination has also resulted in a multiplicity of growing minorities who are infuriated by this insidious dispossession.

DISABLING PROFESSIONS

These minorities already see that they – and all autochthonous cultural life – are threatened by mega-tools which systematically expropriate the environmental conditions that foster individual and group autonomy. And so they quietly determine to fight for the usefulness of their bodies, memories, and skills. Because the rapidly increasing multiplication of imputed needs generates ever new kinds of dependence and ever new categories of modernized poverty, present-day industrial societies take on the character of interdependent conglomerates of bureaucratically stigmatized majorities. Among this great mass of citizens who are crippled by transport, rendered sleepless by schedules, poisoned by hormone therapy, silenced by loudspeakers, sickened by food, a few form minorities of organized and active citizens. Now these are barely beginning to grow and coalesce for public dissidence. Subjectively, these groups are ready to end an age. But to be dispatched, an age needs a name that sticks. I propose to call the mid-twentieth century the Age of Disabling Professions. I choose this designation because it commits those who use it. It exposes the anti-social functions performed by the least challenged providers: educators, physicians, social workers, and scientists. Simultaneously, it indicts the complacency of citizens who have submitted themselves to multi-faceted bondage as clients. To speak about the power of disabling professions shames their victims into recognizing the conspiracy of the life-long student, gynaecological case, or consumer, each with his or her manager. By describing the sixties as an apogee of the problem-solver, one immediately exposes both the inflated conceit of our academic élites and the greedy gullibility of their victims.

But this focus on the makers of the social imagination and the cultural values does more than expose and denounce; by designating the last twenty-five years as the Age of Dominant Professions, one also proposes a strategy. One sees the necessity of going beyond the expert redistribution of wasteful, irrational, and paralyzing commodities, the hallmark of

Radical Professionalism, the conventional wisdom of today's good guys. The strategy demands nothing less than the unmasking of the professional ethos. The credibility of the professional expert, be he scientist, therapist, or executive, is the Achilles' heel of the industrial system. Therefore, only those citizen initiatives and radical technologies that directly challenge the insinuating dominance of disabling professions open the way to freedom for non-hierarchical, community-based competence. The waning of the current professional ethos is a necessary condition for the emergence of a new relationship between needs, contemporary tools, and personal satisfaction. The first step toward this emergence is a sceptical and non-deferential posture of the citizen towards the professional expert. Social reconstruction begins with a doubt raised among citizens.

When I propose the analysis of professional power as the key to social reconstruction, I am usually told that it is a dangerous error to select this phenomenon as the crux for recovery from the industrial system. Is not the shape of the educational, medical, and planning establishments actually the reflection of the distribution of power and privilege of a capitalist élite? Is it not irresponsible to undermine the trust of the man in the street in his scientifically-trained teacher, physician, or economist precisely at the moment when the poor need these trained protectors to gain access to classroom, clinic, and expert? Ought not the industrial system's indictment expose the income of stockholders in drug firms or the perquisites of power-brokers that belong to the new élites? Why spoil the mutual dependence of clients and professional providers, especially when increasingly – as in Cuba or the United States – both tend to come from the same social class? Is it not perverse to denigrate the very people who have painfully acquired the knowledge to recognize and service our needs for welfare? In fact, should not the radically socialist professional leaders be singled out as the most apt leaders in the ongoing task of society of defining and meeting people's 'real' needs in an egalitarian society?

The arguments implicit in these questions are frequently advanced to disrupt and discredit public analysis of the disabling effects of industrial welfare systems which focus on services. Such effects are essentially identical and clearly inevitable, no matter what the political flag under which they are imposed. They incapacitate people's autonomy through forcing them – via legal, environmental, and social changes – to become consumers of care. These rhetorical questions represent a frantic defence of privilege on the part of those élites who might lose income, but would certainly gain status and power if, in a new form of a market-intensive economy, dependence on their services were rendered more equitable.

A further objection to the critique of professional power drives out the devil with Beelzebub. This objection singles out, as the key target for analysis, the defence conglomerates seemingly at the centre of each bureaucratic-industrial society. The developed argument then posits the security forces as the

41

motor behind the contemporary universal regimentation into market-dependent discipline. It identifies as the principal need-makers the armed bureaucracies that have come into being since, under Louis XIV, Richelieu established the first professional police: that is, the professional agencies that are now in charge of weaponry, intelligence, and propaganda. Since Hiroshima, these so-called services appear to be the determinants for research, design production, and employment. They rest upon civilian foundations, such as schooling for discipline, consumer training for the enjoyment of waste, habituation to violent speeds, medical engineering for life in a world-wide shelter, and standardized dependence on issues dispensed by benevolent quartermasters. This line of thought sees state security as the generator of a society's production patterns, and views the civilian economy as, to a large extent, either the military's spin-off or its prerequisite.

If an argument constructed around these notions were valid, how could such a society forego atomic power, no matter how poisonous, oppressive or counter-productive a further energy glut might be? How could a defence-ridden state be expected to tolerate the organization of disaffected citizen groups who unplug their neighbourhoods from consumption to claim the liberty to small-scale use-value-intensive production that happens in an atmosphere of satisfying and joyful austerity? Would not a militarized society soon have to move against need-deserters, brand them as traitors, and, if possible, expose them not just to scorn but to ridicule? Would not a defence-driven society have to stamp out those examples that would lead to non-violent modernity, just at the time when public policy calls for a decentralization of commodity production reminiscent of Mao, and for more rational, equitable, and professionally supervised consumption?

This argument pays undue credit to the military as the source of violence in an industrial state. The assumption that military requirements are to blame for the aggressiveness and destructiveness of advanced industrial society must be exposed as an illusion. No doubt, if it were true that the military had somehow usurped the industrial system, if it had wrenched the various spheres of social endeavour and action away from civilian control, then the present state of militarized politics would have reached a point of no return; at least of no potential for civilian reform. This is in fact the argument made by the brightest of Brazil's military leaders, who see the armed forces as the only legitimate tutor of peaceful industrial pursuit during the rest of this century.

But this is simply not so. The modern industrial state is not a product of the army. Rather, its army is one of the symptoms of its total and consistent orientation. True, the present industrial mode of organization can be traced to military antecedents in Napoleonic times. True, the compulsory education for peasant boys in the 1830s, the universal health care for the industrial proletariat in the 1850s, the growing communications networks of the 1860s, as well as most forms of industrial standardization, are all strategies first introduced into modern societies as military requirements, and only later understood as dignified forms of peaceful, civilian progress. But the fact that *systems* of health, education, and welfare needed a military rationale to be enacted into law, does not mean that they were not thoroughly consistent with the basic thrust of industrial development which, in fact, was never non-violent, peaceful, or respectful of people.

Today, this insight is easier to gain. First, because since Polaris it is no longer possible to distinguish between wartime and peacetime armies and second, because since the War on Poverty, peace is on the war-path. Today, industrial societies are constantly and totally mobilized; they are organized for constant public emergencies; they are shot through with variegated strategies in all sectors; the battlefields of health, education, welfare, and affimative equality are strewn with victims and covered with ruins; citizens' liberties are continually suspended for campaigns against ever newly discovered evils; each year new frontier-dwellers are discovered who must be protected against or cured of some new disease, some previously unknown ignorance. The basic needs that are shaped and imputed by all professional agencies are needs for defence against evils.

Today's professors and social scientists who seek to blame the military for the destructiveness of commodity-intensive societies are people who, in a very clumsy way, are attempting to arrest the erosion of

44

their own legitimacy. They claim that the military pushes the industrial system into its frustrating and destructive state, thereby distracting attention from the profoundly destructive nature of a market-intensive society which drives its citizens into today's wars. Both those who seek to protect professional autonomy against citizen maturity, and those who wish to portray the professional as victim of the militarized state, will be answered by a choice: the direction free citizens wish to go in order to supersede the world-wide crisis.

The waning of the professional age

The illusions that permitted the installation of professions as arbiters of needs are now increasingly visible to common sense. Procedures in the service sector are often understood for what they are – Linus Blankets, or rituals that hide from the provider-consumer-caboodle the disparity and antipathy between the ideal for the sake of which the service is rendered, and the reality that the service creates. Schools that promise equal enlightenment generate unequally degrading meritocracy and life-long dependence on further tutorship; vehicles compel everyone to a flight forward. But the public has not yet clarified the choices. Projects under professional leadership could result in compulsory political creeds (with their accompanying versions of a new fascism), or experiences of citizens could dismiss our hubris as yet another historical collection of neo-Promethean but essentially ephemeral follies. Informed choice requires

45

that we examine the specific role of the professions in determining who in this age got what from whom and why.

To see the present clearly, let us imagine the children who will soon play in the ruins of high-schools, Hiltons – and hospitals. In these professional castles turned cathedrals, built to protect us against ignorance, discomfort, pain, and death, the children of tomorrow will re-enact in their play the delusions of our Age of Professions, as from ancient castles and cathedrals we reconstruct the crusades of knights against sin and the Turk in the Age of Faith. Children in their games will mingle the uniquack which now pollutes our language with archaisms inherited from robber barons and cowboys. I see them addressing each other as chairman and secretary rather than as chief and lord. Hopefully adults will blush when they slip into managerial pidgin with terms such as policy-making, social planning, and problem-solving.

The Age of Professions will be remembered as the time when politics withered, when voters guided by professors entrusted to technocrats the power to legislate needs, the authority to decide who needs what and a monopoly over the means by which these needs shall be met. It will be remembered as the Age of Schooling, when people for one-third of their lives were trained how to accumulate needs on prescription and for the other two-thirds were clients of prestigious pushers who managed their habits. It will be remembered as the age when recreational travel meant a packaged gawk at strangers, and intimacy meant

46

training by Masters and Johnson; when formed opinion was a replay of last night's talk-show, and voting an endorsement to a salesman for more of the same.

Future students will be as much confused by the supposed differences between capitalist and socialist school, health-care, prison or transportation systems as today's students are by the claimed differences between justification by works as opposed to justification by faith in the late Reformation Christian sects. They will also discover that the professional librarians, surgeons, or supermarket designers in poor or socialist countries towards the end of each decade came to keep the same records, use the same tools, and build the same spaces that their colleagues in rich countries had pioneered at the decade's beginning. Archeologists will periodize our life-span not by potsherds but by professional fashions, reflected in the mod-trends of United Nations publications.

It would be pretentious to predict whether this age, when needs were shaped by professional design, will be remembered with a smile or a curse. I hope, of course, that it will be remembered as the night when father went on a binge, dissipated the family fortune, and obligated his children to start anew. Sadly, it will more probably be remembered as the time when a whole generation's frenzied pursuit of impoverishing wealth rendered all freedoms alienable and, after first turning politics into the organized gripes of welfare recipients, extinguished it in expert totalitarianism.

47

Professional dominance

Let us first face the fact that the bodies of specialists that now dominate the creation, adjudication, and satisfaction of needs are a new kind of cartel. And this must be recognized to outflank their developing defences. For we already see the new biocrat hiding behind the benevolent mask of the physician of old; the paedocrat's behavioural aggression is shrugged off as perhaps silly, overzealous care of the concerned teacher; the personnel manager equipped with a psychological arsenal presents himself in the guise of an old-time foreman. The new specialists, who are usually servicers of human needs that their speciality has defined, tend to wear the mask of and to provide some form of care. They are more deeply entrenched than a Byzantine bureaucracy, more international than a world church, more stable than any labour union, endowed with wider competencies than any shaman, and equipped with a tighter hold over those they claim than any mafia.

The new organized specialists must, first, be carefully distinguished from racketeers. Educators, for instance, now tell society what must be learned and can write off as useless what has been learned outside of school. By this kind of monopoly, which enables tyrannical professions to prevent you from shopping elsewhere and from making your own booze, they at first seem to fit the dictionary definition of gangsters. But gangsters, for their own profit, corner a basic necessity by controlling supplies. Educators and doctors and social workers today – as priests and lawyers formerly – gain legal power to create the need that, by law, they alone will be allowed to serve. They turn the modern state into a holding corporation of enterprises that facilitate the operation of their self-certified competencies.

Legalized control over work has taken many different forms: soldiers of fortune refused to fight until they got the licence to plunder; Lysistrata organized female chattels to enforce peace by refusing sex; doctors in Kos conspired by oath to pass trade secrets only to their offspring; guilds set the curricula, prayers, tests, pilgrimages and hazings through which Hans Sachs had to pass before he was permitted to shoe his fellow burghers. In capitalist countries, unions attempt to control who shall work what hours for what pay. All these trade associations are attempts by specialists to determine how their kind of work shall be done, and by whom. But none of these specialists are professionals in the sense that doctors, for instance, are today. Today's domineering professionals, of whom physicians provide the most striking and painful example, go further: they decide what shall be made, for whom, and how it shall be administered. They claim special, incommunicable knowledge, not just about the way things are and are to be made, but also about the reasons why their services ought to be needed. Merchants sell you the goods they stock. Guildsmen guarantee quality. Some craftspeople tailor their product to your measure or fancy. Professionals however, tell you what you need.

They claim the power to prescribe. They not only advertise what is good, but ordain what is right. Neither income, long training, delicate tasks, nor social standing is the mark of the professional. Their income can be low or taxed away, their training compressed into weeks instead of years; their status can approach that of the oldest profession. Rather, what counts is the professional's authority to define a person as client, to determine that person's need, and to hand that person a prescription which defines this new social role. Unlike the hookers of old, the modern professional is not one who sells what others give for free, but rather one who decides what ought to be sold and must not be given for free.

There is a further distinction between professional power and that of other occupations: professional power springs from a different source. A guild, a union, or a gang forces respect for its interest and rights by a strike, blackmail, or overt violence. In contrast, a profession, like a priesthood, holds power by concession from an élite whose interests it props up. As a priesthood offers the way to salvation in the train of an anointed king, so a profession interprets, protects, and supplies a special this-worldly interest to the constituency of modern rulers. Professional power is a specialized form of the privilege to prescribe what is right for others and what they therefore need. It is the source of prestige and control within the industrial state. This kind of professional power could, of course, come into existence only in societies where élite membership itself is legitimated, if not acquired, by professional status: a society where governing élites are attributed a unique kind of objectivity in defining the moral status of a lack. It fits like a glove the age in which even access to parliament, the house of commons, is overwhelmingly limited to those who have acquired the title of master by accumulating knowledge stock in some college. Professional autonomy and licence, in defining the needs of society are the logical forms that oligarchy takes in a political culture that has replaced the means-test by knowledge-stock certificates issued by schools. The professions' power over the work their members do is thus distinct in both scope and origin.

Towards professional tyranny

Professional power has also, recently, so changed in degree that two animals of entirely different colours now go by the same name. For instance, the practicing and experimenting health scientist consistently evades critical analysis by dressing up in the clothes of yesterday's family doctor. The wandering physician became the medical doctor when he left commerce in drugs to the pharmacist and kept for himself the power to prescribe them. At that moment, he acquired a new kind of authority by uniting three roles in one person: the sapiential authority to advise, instruct, and direct; the moral authority that makes its acceptance not just useful but obligatory; and the charismatic authority that allows the physician to appeal to some supreme interest of his clients that not only outranks conscience but sometimes even the *raison d'état.* This kind of doctor, of course, still exists, but within a modern medical system he is a figure out of the past. A new kind of health scientist is now much more common. He increasingly deals more with cases than with persons; he deals with the breakdowns that he can perceive in the case, rather than with the complaint of the individual; he protects society's interest rather than the person's. The authorities that, during the liberal age, had coalesced in the individual practitioner in his treatment of a patient are now claimed by the professional corporation in the service of the state. This entity now carves out for itself a social mission.

Only during the last twenty-five years has medicine turned from a liberal into a dominant profession by obtaining the power to indicate what constitutes a health need for people in general. Health specialists as a corporation have acquired the authority to determine what health care must be provided to society at large. It is no longer the individual professional who imputes a 'need' to the individual client, but a corporate agency that imputes a need to entire classes of people, and then claims the mandate to test the complete population in order to identify all who belong to the group of potential patients. And what happens in health care is thoroughly consistent with other domains. New pundits jump on the bandwagon of the therapeutic care-provider: educators, social workers, the military, town-planners, judges, policemen, and their ilk have obviously made it. They enjoy wide autonomy in creating the diagnostic tools by which they then catch their clients for treatment. Dozens of other need-creators try: international bankers 'diagnose' the ills of an African country and then induce it to swallow the prescribed treatment, even though the 'patient' might die; security specialists evaluate the loyalty risk in a citizen and then extinguish his private sphere; dog-catchers sell themselves to the public as pest controllers, and claim a monopoly over the lives of stray dogs. The only way to prevent the escalation of needs is a fundamental, political exposure of those illusions that legitimize dominating professions.

Many professions are so well established that they not only exercise tutelage over the citizen-become-client, but also determine the shape of his world-become-ward. The language in which he perceives himself, his perception of rights and freedoms, and his awareness of needs all derive from professional hegemony.

The difference between craftsman, liberal professional, and the new technocrat can be clarified by comparing the typical reaction of people who neglect their respective advice. If you did not take the craftsman's advice, you were a fool. If you did not take liberal counsel, society blamed you. Now the profession or the government may be blamed when you escape from the care that your lawyer, teacher, surgeon, or shrink has decided upon for you. Under the pretense of meeting needs better and on a more equitable basis, the service-professional has mutated into a crusading philanthropist. The nutritionist prescribes the 'right' formula for the infant, and the

53

psychiatrist the 'right' anti-depressant, and the schoolmaster – now acting with the fuller power of 'educator' – feels entitled to push his method between you and anything you want to learn. Each new speciality in service production thrives only when the public has accepted and the law has endorsed a new perception of what ought not to exist. Schools expanded in a moralizing crusade against illiteracy, once illiteracy had been defined as an evil. Maternity wards mushroomed to do away with home births.

Professionals claim a monopoly over the definition of deviance and the remedies needed. For example, lawyers assert that they alone have the competence and the legal right to provide assistance in divorce. If you devise a kit for do-it-yourself divorce, you find yourself in a double bind: if you are not a lawyer, you are liable of practice without a license; if you are a member of the bar, you can be expelled for unprofessional behaviour. Professionals also claim secret knowledge about human nature and its weaknesses, knowledge they are also mandated to apply. Gravediggers, for example, did not become members of a profession by calling themselves morticians, by obtaining college credentials, by raising their incomes, or by getting rid of the odour attached to their trade by electing one of themselves president of the Lion's Club. Morticians formed a profession, a dominant and disabling one, when they acquired the muscle to have the police stop your burial if you are not embalmed and boxed by them. In any area where a human need can be imagined, these new disabling professions claim that they are the exclusive experts of the public good.

Professions as a new clergy

The transformation of a liberal profession into a dominant one is equivalent to the legal establishment of a church. Physicians transmogrified into biocrats, teachers into gnosocrats, morticians into thanatocrats, are much closer to state-supported clergies than to trade associations. The professional as teacher of the current brand of scientific orthodoxy acts as theologian. As moral entrepreneur, he acts the role of priest: he creates the need for his mediation. As crusading helper, he acts the part of the missionary and hunts down the underprivileged. As inquisitor, he outlaws the unorthodox – he imposes his solutions on the recalcitrants who refuse to recognize that they are a problem. This multi-faceted investiture with the task of relieving a specific inconvenience of man's estate turns each profession into the analogue of an established cult. The public acceptance of domineering professions is thus essentially a political event. The new profession creates a new hierarchy, new clients and outcasts, and a new strain on the budget. But, also, each new establishment of professional legitimacy means that the political tasks of lawmaking, judicial review, and executive power lose more of their proper character and independence. Public affairs pass from the layperson's elected peers into the hands of a self-accrediting élite.

When medicine recently outgrew its liberal restraints, it invaded legislation by establishing public

55

norms. Physicians had always determined what constitutes disease; dominant medicine now determines what diseases society shall not tolerate. Medicine has invaded the courts. Physicians had always diagnosed who is sick; dominant medicine, however, brands those who must be treated. Liberal practitioners prescribed a cure: dominant medicine has public powers of correction; it decides what shall be done with or to the sick. In a democracy, the power to make laws, execute them, and achieve public justice must derive from the citizens themselves. This citizen control over the key powers has been restricted, weakened, and sometimes abolished by the rise of church-like professions. Government by a congress that bases its decisions on expert opinions of such professions might be government for, but never by, the people. This is not the place to investigate the intent with which political rule has thus been weakened; it is sufficient to indicate the professional disqualification of lay opinion as a necessary condition for this subversion.

Citizen liberties are grounded in the rule that excludes hearsay from testimony on which public decisions are based. What people can see for themselves and interpret is the common ground for binding rules. Opinions, beliefs, inferences, or persuasions ought not to stand when in conflict with the eye-witness – ever. Expert élites could become dominant professions only by a piecemeal erosion and final reversal of this rule. In the legislature and courts, the rule against hearsay evidence is now, *de facto,* suspended in favour of the opinions profferred by the members of these self-accredited élites.

But let us not confuse the public use of expert factual knowledge with a profession's corporate exercise of normative judgment. When a craftsman, such as a gunmaker, was called into court as an expert to reveal to the jury the secrets of his trade, he apprenticed the jury to his craft on the spot. He demonstrated visibly from which barrel the bullet had come. Today, most experts play a different role. The dominant professional provides jury or legislature with his fellow-initiate's opinion, rather than with factual evidence and a skill. He calls for a suspension of the hearsay rule and inevitably undermines the rule of law. Thus, democratic power is ineluctably abridged.

The hegemony of imputed needs

Professions could not have become dominant and disabling unless people were ready to experience as a lack that which the expert imputed to them as a need. Their mutual dependence as tutor and charge has become resistant to analysis because it has been obscured by corrupted language. Good old words have been made into branding irons that claim wardship for experts over home, shop, store, and the space or ether between them. Language, the most fundamental of commons, is thus polluted by twisted strands of jargon, each under the control of another profession. The disseizin of words, the depletion of ordinary language and its degradation into bureaucratic terminology, parallel in a more intimately

57

debasing manner that particular form of environmental degradation that dispossesses people of their usefulness unless they are gainfully employed. Possible changes in design, attitudes, and laws that would retrench professional dominance cannot be proposed unless we become more sensitive to the misnomers behind which this dominance hides.

When I learned to speak, 'problems' existed only in mathematics or chess; 'solutions' were saline or legal, and 'need' was mainly used as a verb. The expressions, 'I have a problem', or, 'I have a need', both sounded silly. As I grew into my teens and Hitler worked at solutions, the 'social problem' also spread. 'Problem' children of ever newer shades were discovered among the poor as social workers learned to brand their prey and to standardize their 'needs'. 'Need', used as a noun, became the fodder on which professions fattened into dominance. Poverty was modernized. Management translated poverty from an experience into a measure. The poor became the needy.

During the second half of my life, to be 'needy' became respectable. Computable and imputable needs moved up the social ladder. It ceased to be a sign of poverty to have needs. Income opened new registers of need. Spock, Comfort, and the vulgarizers of Nader trained laymen to shop for solutions to problems they learned to cook up according to professional recipes. Education qualified graduates to climb ever more rarefied heights and implant and cultivate there ever newer strains of hybridized needs.

Prescriptions increased and competences shrank. For example, in medicine, ever more pharmacologically active drugs went on prescription, and people lost their will and ability to cope with indisposition or even with discomfort. In American supermarkets, where it is estimated that about 1500 new products appear each year, less than 20 per cent survive more than one year on the shelves, the remainder, having proved unsellable, fadish, risky, unprofitable, or obsolete competitors to new models. Therefore, consumers are forced to seek guidance from professional consumer protectors.

Furthermore, the rapid turnover of products renders wants shallow and plastic. Paradoxically, then, high aggregate consumption resulting from engineered needs fosters growing consumer indifference to specific, potentially felt wants. Increasingly, needs are created by the advertising slogan and by purchases made by order from registrar, beautician, gynaecologist, and dozens of other prescribing diagnosticians. The need to be formally taught how to need, be this by advertising, prescription, or guided discussion in the collective or in the commune, appears in any culture where decisions and actions are no longer the result of personal experience in satisfaction, and the adaptive consumer cannot but substitute learned for felt needs. As people become apt pupils in learning how to need, the ability to shape wants from experienced satisfaction becomes a rare competence of the very rich or the seriously under-supplied. As needs are broken down into ever smaller component parts, each

59

managed by an appropriate specialist, the consumer experiences difficulty in integrating the separate offerings of his various tutors into a meaningful whole that could be desired with commitment and possessed with pleasure. The income managers, life-style counsellors, consciousness raisers, academic advisers, food-fad experts, sensitivity developers, and others like them clearly perceive the new possibilities for management and move in to match packaged commodities to the splintered needs.

Used as a noun, 'need' is the individual offspring of a professional pattern; it is a plastic-foam replica of the mould in which professionals cast their staple; it is the advertised shape of the brood cells out of which consumers are produced. To be ignorant or unconvinced of one's own needs has become the unforgivable anti-social act. The good citizen is one who imputes standardized needs to himself with such conviction that he drowns out any desire for alternatives, much less the renunciation of need.

When I was born, before Stalin and Hitler and Roosevelt came to power, only the rich, hypochondriacs, and members of élite unions spoke of their need for medical care when their temperatures rose. Doctors then, in response, could not do much more than grandmothers had done. In medicine the first mutation of needs came with sulfa drugs and antibiotics. As the control of infections became a simple and effective routine, drugs went more and more on prescription. Assignment of the sick-role became a medical monopoly. The person who felt ill had to go to the clinic to be labelled with a disease-name and be legitimately declared a member of the minority of the so-called sick: people were excused from work, entitled to help, put under doctor's orders, and were enjoined to heal in order to become useful again. Paradoxically, as pharmacological technique – tests and drugs – became so predictable and cheap that one could have dispensed with the physician, society enacted laws and police regulations to restrict the free use of those procedures that science had simplified, and placed them on the prescription list.

The second mutation of medical needs happened when the sick ceased to be a minority. Today, few people eschew doctors' orders for any length of time. In Italy, the United States, France, or Belgium, one out of every two citizens is being watched simultaneously by several health professionals who treat, advise, or at least observe him or her. The object of such specialized care is, more often than not, a condition of teeth, womb, emotions, blood pressure, or hormone levels that the patient himself does not feel. Patients are no more in the minority. Now, the minority are those deviants who somehow escape from any and all patient-roles. This minority is made up of the poor, the peasants, the recent immigrants, and sundry others who, sometimes of their own volition, have gone medically AWOL. Just twenty years ago, it was a sign of normal health – which was assumed to be good – to get along without a doctor. The same status of non-patient is now indicative of poverty or dissidence. Even the status of the hypochondriac has changed. For the doctor in the forties, this was the label applied to the gate-crashers in his office – the designation reserved for the imaginary sick. Now, doctors refer to the minority who flee them by the same name: hypochondriacs are the imaginary healthy. To be plugged into a professional system as a life-long client is no longer a stigma that sets apart the disabled person from citizens at large. We now live in a society organized for deviant majorities and their keepers. To be an active client of several professionals provides you with a well-defined place within the realm of consumers for the sake of whom our society functions. Thus, the transformation of medicine from a liberal consulting profession into a dominant, disabling profession has immeasurably increased the number of the needy.

At this critical moment, imputed needs move into a third mutation. They coalesce into what the experts call a multi-disciplinary problem necessitating, therefore, a multi-professional solution. First, the proliferation of commodities, each tending to turn into a requirement, has effectively trained the consumer to need on command. Next, the progressive fragmentation of needs into even smaller and unconnected parts made the client dependent on professional judgment for the blending of his needs into a meaningful whole. The auto industry provides a good example. By the end of the sixties, the advertised optional equipment needed to make a basic Ford desirable had been multiplied immensely. But contrary to the customer's expectations, this 'optional' flim-flam is in fact installed on the assembly line of the Detroit factory, and the shopper in Plains is left with a choice between a few packaged samples that are shipped at random: he can either buy the convertible that he wants but with the green seats he hates, or he can humour his girlfriend with leopardskin seats – at the cost of buying an unwanted paisley hard top.

Finally, the client is trained to need a team approach to receive what his guardians consider 'satisfactory treatment'. Personal services that improve the consumer illustrate the point. Therapeutic affluence has exhausted the available life-time of many whom service professionals diagnose as standing in need of more. The intensity of the service economy has made the time needed for the consumption of pedagogical, medical and social treatments increasingly scarce. Time scarcity may soon turn into the major obstacle for the consumption of prescribed, and often publicly financed, services. Signs of such scarcity become evident from one's early years. Already in kindergarten, the child is subjected to management by a team made up of such specialists as the allergist, speech pathologist, paediatrician, child psychologist, social worker, physical education instructor and teacher. By forming such a paedocratic team, many different professionals attempt to share the time that has become the major limiting factor to the imputation of further needs. For the adult, it is not the school but the work-place where the packaging of services focuses. The personnel manager, labour educator, in-service trainer, insurance planner, consciousness raiser find it more profitable to share the worker's time than compete for it. A need-less citizen would be highly suspicious. People are told that they need their jobs, not so much for the money as for the services they get. The commons are extinguished and replaced by a new placenta built of funnels that deliver professional services. Life is paralyzed in permanent intensive care.

[3]

ENABLING DISTINCTIONS

The disabling of the citizen through professional dominance is completed through the power of illusion. Hopes of religious salvation are displaced by expectations that centre on the state as supreme manager of professional services. Each of many special priesthoods claims competence to define public issues in terms of specific serviceable problems. The acceptance of this claim legitimates the docile recognition of imputed lacks on the part of the layman, whose world turns into an echo-chamber of engineered and managed needs. This dominance, the satisfaction of self-defined preference, is sacrificed to the fulfilment of educated needs and is reflected in the skyline of the city. Professional buildings look down on the crowds that shuttle between them in a continual pilgrimage to the new cathedrals of health, education, and welfare. Healthy homes are transformed into hygienic apartments where one cannot be born, cannot be sick, and cannot die decently. Not only are helpful neighbours a vanishing species, but also liberal doctors who make house calls. Work places fit for apprenticeship turn into opaque mazes of corridors that permit access only to functionaries equipped with 'identities' in mica holders pinned to their lapels. A world designed for service deliveries is the utopia of citizens turned into welfare recipients.

The prevailing addiction to imputable needs on the part of the rich, and the paralyzing fascination with needs on the part of the poor, would indeed be irreversible if people actually fitted the calculus of needs. But this is not so. Beyond a certain level of intensity, medicine engenders helplessness and disease; education turns into the major generator of a disabling division of labour; fast transportation systems turn urbanized people for about one-sixth of their waking hours into passengers, and for an equal amount of time into members of the road gang that works to pay Ford, Esso, and the highway department. The threshold at which medicine, education, and transportation turn into counterproductive tools has been reached in all the countries of the world with per capita incomes comparable at least to those

66

prevalent in Cuba. In all countries examined, and contrary to the illusions propagated by the orthodoxies of both East and West, this specific counterproductivity bears no relation to the kind of school, vehicle, or health organization now used. It sets in when the capital-intensity of the production process passes a critical threshold.

Our major institutions have acquired the uncanny power to subvert the very purposes for which they were originally engineered and financed. Under the rule of our most prestigious professions, our institutional tools have as their principal product paradoxical counterproductivity – the systematic disabling of the citizenry. A city built around wheels becomes inappropriate for feet, and no increase of wheels can overcome the engineered immobility of such cripples. Autonomous action is paralyzed by a surfeit of commodities and treatments. But this does not represent simply a net loss of satisfactions that do not happen to fit into the industrial age. The impotence to produce use-values ultimately renders counterpurposive the very commodities meant to replace them. The car, the doctor, the school, and the manager are then commodities that have turned into destructive nuisances for the consumer, and retain net value only for the provider of services.

Why are there no rebellions against the coalescence of late industrial society into one huge disabling service delivery system? The chief explanation must be sought in the illusion-generating power that these same systems possess. Besides doing technical things

67

to body and mind, professionally attended institutions function also as powerful rituals which generate credence in the things their managers promise. Besides teaching Johnny to read, schools also teach him that learning from teachers is 'better', and that, without compulsory schools, fewer books would be read by the poor. Besides providing locomotion, the bus, just as much as the sedan, reshapes the environment and puts walking out of step. Besides providing help in avoiding taxes, lawyers also convey the notion that laws solve problems. An ever growing part of our major institutions' functions is the cultivation and maintenance of three sets of illusions which turn the citizen into a client to be saved by experts.

Congestion versus paralysis

The first enslaving illusion is the idea that people are born to be consumers and that they can attain any of their goals by purchasing goods and services. This illusion is due to an educated blindness to the worth of use-values in the total economy. In none of the economic models serving as national guidelines is there a variable to account for non-marketable use-values any more than there is a variable for nature's perennial contribution. Yet there is no economy that would not collapse immediately if use-value production contracted beyond a point; for example, if home-making were done only for wages, or intercourse engaged in only at a fee. What people do or make but will not or cannot put up for sale is as immeasurable

68

and as invaluable for the economy as the oxygen they breathe.

The illusion that economic models can ignore use-values springs from the assumption that those activities which we designate by intransitive verbs can be indefinitely replaced by institutionally defined staples referred to as nouns: 'education' substituted for 'I learn'; 'health care' for 'I heal'; transportation for 'I move'; 'television' for 'I play'.

The confusion of personal and standardized values has spread throughout most domains. Under professional leadership, use-values are dissolved, rendered obsolete, and finally deprived of their distinctive nature. Love and institutional care become coterminous. Ten years of running a farm can be thrown into a pedagogical mixer and made equivalent to a high school degree. Things picked up at random and hatched in the freedom of the street are added as 'educational experience' to things funneled into pupils' heads. The knowledge accountants seem unaware that the two activities, like oil and water, mix only as long as they are osterized by an educator's perception. Gangs of crusading need-catchers could not continue to tax us, nor could they spend our resources on their tests, networks, and other nostrums if we did not remain paralyzed by this kind of greedy belief.

The usefulness of staples, or packaged commodities, is intrinsically limited by two boundaries that must not be confused. First, queues will sooner or later stop the operation of any system that produces needs faster than the corresponding commodity and, second, dependence on commodities will sooner or later so determine needs that the autonomous production of a functional analogue will be paralyzed. The usefulness of commodities is limited by *congestion* and *paralysis*. Congestion and paralysis are both results of escalation in any sector of production, albeit results of a very different kind. Congestion, which is a measure of the degree to which staples get in their own way, explains why mass transportation by private car in Manhattan would be useless; it does not explain why people work hard to buy and insure cars that cannot move them. Even less does congestion alone explain why people become so dependent on vehicles that they are paralyzed and just cannot take to their feet.

People become prisoners to time-consuming acceleration, stupefying education and sick-making medicine because beyond a certain threshold of intensity, dependence on a bill of industrial and professional goods destroys human potential, and does so in a specific way. Only up to a point can commodities replace what people make or do on their own. Only within limits can exchange-values satisfactorily replace use-values. Beyond this point, further production serves the interests of the professional producer – who has imputed the need to the consumer – and leaves the consumer befuddled and giddy, albeit richer. Needs satisfied rather than merely fed must be determined to a significant degree by the pleasure that is derived from the remembrance of personal autonomous action. There are boundaries beyond

70

which commodities cannot be multiplied without disabling their consumer for this self-affirmation in action.

Packages alone inevitably frustrate the consumer when their delivery paralyzes him or her. The measure of well-being in a society is thus never an equation in which these two modes of production are matched; it is always a balance that results when use-values and commodities fruitfully mesh in synergy. Only up to a point can heteronomous production of a commodity enhance and complement the autonomous production of the corresponding personal purpose. Beyond this point, the synergy between the two modes of production paradoxically turns against the purpose for which both use-value and commodity were intended. Occasionally, this is not clearly seen because the mainstream ecology movement tends to obscure the point. For example, atomic energy reactors have been widely criticized because their radiation is a threat, or because they foster technocratic controls. So far, however, only very few have dared to criticize them because they add to the energy glut. The paralysis of human action by socially destructive energy quanta has not yet been accepted as an argument for reducing the call for energy. Similarly, the inexorable limits to growth that are built into any service agency are still widely ignored. And yet it ought to be evident that the institutionalization of health care tends to make people into unhealthy marionettes, and that life long education fosters a culture of programmed people.

Ecology will provide guidelines for a feasible form of modernity only when it is recognized that a man-made environment designed for commodities reduces personal aliveness to the point where the commodities themselves lose their value as means for personal satisfaction. Without this insight, industrial technology that was cleaner and less aggressive would be used for now-impossible levels of frustrating enrichment.

It would be a mistake to attribute counterproductivity essentially to the negative externalities of economic growth, to exhaustion, pollution and various forms of congestion. This mistake would lead to confusing the congestion by which things get into his way, with the paralysis of the person who can no more exercise his autonomy in an environment designed for things.

The fundamental reason why market intensity leads to counterproductivity must be sought in the relationship between the monopoly of commodities and human needs. This monopoly extends beyond its usual meaning. A commercial monopoly merely corners the market for one brand of whisky or car. An industry-wide cartel can restrict freedom further: it can corner all mass transportation in favour of internal combustion engines, as General Motors did when it purchased the Los Angeles trolleys. You can escape the first by sticking to rum and the second by purchasing a bicycle. I use the term 'radical monopoly' to designate something else: the substitution of an industrial product or a professional service for a useful activity in which people engage or would like to engage. A radical monopoly paralyzes autonomous action in favour of professional deliveries. The more completely vehicles dislocate people, the more traffic managers will be needed and the more powerless people will be to walk home. This radical monopoly would accompany high-speed traffic even if motors were powered by sunshine and vehicles were spun of air. The longer each person is in the grip of education, the less time and inclination he has for browsing and exploration. At some point in every domain, the amount of goods delivered so degrades the environment for personal action that the possible synergy between use-values and commodities turns negative. Paradoxical, or specific, counterproductivity sets in. I will use this term whenever the impotence resulting from the substitution of a commodity for a value in use turns this commodity into a dis-value in the pursuit of the satisfaction it was meant to provide.

Industrial versus convivial tools

Man ceases to be recognizable as one of his kind when he can no longer shape his own needs by the more or less competent use of those tools that his culture provides. Throughout history, most tools were labour-intensive means that could be used to satisfy the user of the tool, and were used in domestic production. Only marginally were shovels or hammers used to produce pyramids or a surplus for gift-exchange, and even more rarely to produce things for the market. Occasions for the extraction of profits were limited.

73

Most work was done to create use-values not destined for exchange. But technological progress has been consistently applied to develop a very different kind of tool: it has pressed the tool primarily into the production of marketable staples. At first, during the industrial revolution, the new technology reduced the worker on the job to a Charlie Chaplin of *Modern Times*. At this early stage, however, the industrial mode of production did not yet paralyze people when they were off the job. Now women or men, who have come to depend almost entirely on deliveries of standardized fragments produced by tools operated by anonymous others, have ceased to find the same direct satisfaction in the use of tools that stimulated the evolution of man and his cultures. Although their needs and their consumption have multiplied many times, their satisfaction in handling tools has become rare, and they have ceased to live a life for which the organism acquired its form. At best, they barely survive, even though they do so surrounded by glitter. Their life-span has become a chain of needs that have been met for the sake of ulterior striving for satisfaction. Ultimately man-the-passive-consumer loses even the ability to discriminate between living and survival. The gamble on insurance and the gleeful expectation of rations and therapies take the place of enjoyment. In such company, it becomes easy to forget that satisfaction and joy can result only as long as personal aliveness and engineered provisions are kept in balance while a goal is pursued.

The delusion that tools in the service of market-

74

orientated institutions can with impunity destroy the conditions for convivial and personally manageable means permits the extinction of 'aliveness' by conceiving of technological progress as a kind of engineering product that licences more professional domination. This delusion says that tools, in order to become more efficient in the pursuit of a specific purpose, inevitably become more complex and inscrutable: one thinks of cockpits and cranes. Therefore, it seems that modern tools necessarily require special operators who are highly trained and who alone can be securely trusted. Actually, just the opposite is usually true, and ought to be so. As techniques multiply and become more specific, their use often requires less complex judgments. They no longer require that trust on the part of the client on which the autonomy of the liberal professional, and even that of the craftsman, was built. However far medicine has advanced, only a tiny fraction of the total volume of demonstrably useful medical services requires advanced training in an intelligent person. From a social point of view, we ought to reserve the designation 'technical progress' to instances in which new tools expand the capacity and the effectiveness of a wider range of people, especially when new tools permit more autonomous production of use-values.

There is nothing inevitable about the expanding professional monopoly over new technology. The great inventions of the last hundred years, such as new metals, ball-bearings, some building materials, electronics, some tests and remedies, are capable of increasing the power of both the heteronomous and the autonomous modes of production. In fact, however, most new technology has not been incorporated into convivial equipment, but into institutional packages and complexes. The professionals rather consistently have used industrial production to establish a radical monopoly by means of technology's obvious power to serve its manager. Counterproductivity due to the paralysis of use-value production is fostered by this notion of technological progress.

There is no simple 'technological imperative' which requires that ball-bearings be used in motorized vehicles or that electronics be used to control the brain. The institutions of high-speed traffic and of mental health are not the necessary result of ball-bearings or electronics. Their functions are determined by the needs they are supposed to serve – needs that are overwhelmingly imputed and reinforced by disabling professions. This is a point that the young Turks in the professions seem to overlook when they justify their institutional allegiance by presenting themselves as the publicly appointed ministers of technological progress that must be domesticated.

The same subservience to the idea of progress conceives of engineering principally as a contribution to institutional effectiveness. Scientific research is highly financed, but only if it can be applied for military use or for further professional domination. Alloys which make bicycles both stronger and lighter are a fall-out of research designed to make jets faster and weapons deadlier. But the results of most research go solely into industrial tools, thus making already huge machines even more complex and inscrutable. Because of this bias on the part of scientists and engineers, a major trend is strengthened: needs for autonomous action are precluded, while those for the acquisition of commodities are multiplied. Convivial tools which facilitate the individual's enjoyment of use-values – without or with only minimal supervision by policemen, physicians, or inspectors – are polarized at two extremes: poor Asian workers and rich students and professors are the two kinds of people who ride bicycles. Perhaps without being conscious of their good fortune, both enjoy being free from this second illusion.

Recently, some groups of professionals, government agencies, and international organizations have begun to explore, develop, and advocate small-scale, intermediate technology. These efforts might be interpreted as an attempt to avoid the more obvious vulgarities of a technological imperative. But most of the new technology designed for self-help in health care, education, or home building is only an alternative model of high-intensity dependence commodities. For example, experts are asked to design new medicine cabinets that allow people to follow the doctor's orders over the telephone. Women are taught to determine themselves how ripe their breasts are for useless amputation by the surgeon. Cubans are given paid leaves from work to erect their pre-fabricated houses. The enticing prestige of professional products as they become cheaper ends by making rich and poor

77

more alike. Both Bolivians and Swedes feel equally backward, underprivileged, and exploited to the degree that they learn without the supervision of certified teachers, keep healthy without the check-ups of a physician, and move about without a motorized crutch.

Liberties versus rights

The third disabling illusion looks to experts for limits to growth. Entire populations socialized to need on command are assumed ready to be told what they do not need. The same multinational agents that for a generation imposed an international standard of bookkeeping, deodorants, and energy consumption on rich and poor alike now sponsor the Club of Rome. Obediently, UNESCO gets into the act and trains experts in the regionalization of imputed needs. For their own imputed good, the rich are thereby programmed to pay for more costly professional dominance at home and to provide the poor with assigned needs of a cheaper and tighter brand. The brightest of the new professionals see clearly that growing scarcity pushes controls over needs ever upward. The central planning of output-optimal decentralization has become the most prestigious job of the late seventies. But what is not yet recognized is that this new illusory salvation by professionally decreed limits confuses liberties and rights.

In each of the seven United Nations-defined world regions a new clergy is being trained to preach the appropriate style of austerity drafted by the new need-designers. Consciousness raisers roam through local communities inciting people to meet the decentralized production goals that have been assigned to them. Milking the family goat was a liberty until more ruthless planning made it a duty to contribute the yield to the GNP.

The synergy of autonomous and heteronomous production is reflected in society's balance of liberties and rights. Liberties protect use-values as rights protect the access to commodities. And just as commodities can extinguish the possibility of producing use-values and turn into impoverishing wealth, so the professional definition of rights can extinguish liberties and establish a tyranny that smothers people underneath their rights.

The confusion is revealed with special clarity when one considers the experts on health. Health encompasses two aspects: liberties and rights. It designates the area of autonomy within which a person exercises control over his own biological states and over the conditions of his immediate environment. Simply stated, health is identical with the degree of lived freedom. Therefore, those concerned with the public good should work to guarantee the equitable distribution of health as freedom which, in turn, depends on environmental conditions that only organized political efforts can achieve. Beyond a certain level of intensity, professional health care, however equitably distributed, will smother health-as-freedom. In this fundamental sense, the care of health is a matter of well-protected liberty.

79

As is evident, such a notion of health implies a principled commitment to inalienable freedoms. To understand this, one must distinguish clearly between civil liberty and civil rights. The liberty to act without restraint from government has a wider scope than the civil rights the state may enact to guarantee that people will have equal powers to obtain certain goods and services.

Civil liberties ordinarily do not force others to act in accord with one's own wishes. I have the freedom to speak and publish my opinion, but no specific newspaper is obliged to print it, nor are fellow citizens required to read it. I am free to paint as I see beauty, but no museum has to buy my canvas. At the same time, however, the state as guarantor of liberty can and does enact laws that protect the equal rights without which its members would not enjoy their freedoms. Such rights give meaning and reality to equality, while liberties give possibility and shape to freedom. One certain way to extinguish the freedoms to speak, to learn, to heal, or to care is to delimit them by transmogrifying civil rights into civic duties. The precise character of this third illusion is to believe that the publicly sponsored pursuit of rights leads inevitably to the protection of liberties. In reality, as society gives professionals the legitimacy to define rights, citizen freedoms evaporate.

[4]

EQUITY
IN   USEFUL   UNEMPLOYMENT

At present, every new need that is professionally
certified translates sooner or later into a right. The
political pressure for the enactment of each right
generates new jobs and commodities. Each new
commodity degrades an activity by which people so
far have been able to cope on their own; each new job
takes away legitimacy from work so far done by the
unemployed. The power of professions to measure
what shall be good, right, and done warps the desire,
willingness, and ability of the 'common' man to live
within his measure

81

As soon as all law students currently registered at United States law schools are graduated, the number of United States lawyers will increase by about 50 per cent. Judicare will complement Medicare, as legal insurance increasingly turns into the kind of necessity that medical insurance is now. When the right of the citizen to a lawyer has been established, settling the dispute in the pub will be branded unenlightened or anti-social, as home births are now. Already the right of each citizen of Detroit to live in a home that has been professionally wired turns the auto-electrician who installs his own plugs into a lawbreaker. The loss of one liberty after another to be useful when out of a job or outside professional control is the unnamed, but also the most resented experience that comes with modernized poverty. By now the most significant privilege of high social status might well be some vestige of freedom for useful unemployment that is increasingly denied to the great majority. The insistence on the right to be taken care of and supplied has almost turned into the right of industries and professions to conquer clients, to supply them with their product, and by their deliveries to obliterate the environmental conditions that make unemployed activities useful. Thus, for the time being, the struggle for an equitable distribution of the time and the power to be useful to self and others outside employment or the draft has been effectively paralyzed. Work done off the paid job is looked down upon if not ignored. Autonomous activity threatens the employment level, generates deviance, and detracts

82

from the GNP: therefore it is only improperly called 'work'. Labour no longer means effort or toil but the mysterious mate wedded to productive investments in plant. Work no longer means the creation of a value perceived by the worker but mainly a job, which is a social relationship. Unemployment means sad idleness, rather than the freedom to do things that are useful for oneself or for one's neighbour. An active woman who runs a house and brings up children and takes in those of others is distinguished from a woman who 'works', no matter how useless or damaging the product of this work might be. Activity, effort, achievement, or service outside a hierarchical relationship and unmeasured by professional standards, threatens a commodity-intensive society. The generation of use-values that escape effective measurement limits not only the need for more commodities but also the jobs that create them and the paycheques needed to buy them.

What counts in a market-intensive society is not the effort to please or the pleasure that flows from that effort but the coupling of the labour force with capital. What counts is not the achievement of satisfaction that flows from action but the status of the social relationship that commands production – that is, the job, situation, post, or appointment. In the Middle Ages there was no salvation outside the Church, and the theologians had a hard time explaining what God did with those pagans who were visibly virtuous or saintly. Similarly, in contemporary society effort is not productive unless it is done at the behest of a boss, and economists have a hard time dealing with the obvious usefulness of people when they are outside the corporate control of a corporation, volunteer agency, or labour camp. Work is productive, respectable, worthy of the citizen only when the work process is planned, monitored, and controlled by a professional agent, who insures that the work meets a certified need in a standardized fashion. In an advanced industrial society it becomes almost impossible to seek, even to imagine, unemployment as a condition for autonomous, useful work. The infrastructure of society is so arranged that only the job gives access to the tools of production, and this monopoly of commodity production over the generation of use-values turns even more stringent as the state takes over. Only with a license may you teach a child; only at a clinic may you set a broken bone. Housework, handicrafts, subsistence agriculture, radical technology, learning exchanges, and the like are degraded into activities for the idle, the unproductive, the very poor, or the very rich. A society that fosters intense dependence on commodities thus turns its unemployed into either its poor or its dependents. In 1945, for each American Social Security recipient there were still 35 workers on the job. In 1977, 3.2 employed workers have to support one such retiree, who is himself dependent on many more services than his retired grandfather could have imagined.

Henceforth the quality of a society and of its culture will depend on the status of its unemployed:

84

will they be the most representative productive citizens, or will they be dependants? The choice or crisis again seems clear: advanced industrial society can degenerate into a holding operation harking back to the dream of the sixties; into a well-rationed distribution system that doles out decreasing commodities and jobs and trains its citizens for more standardized consumption and more powerless work. This is the attitude reflected in the policy proposals of most governments at present, from Germany to China, albeit a fundamental difference in degree: the richer the country, the more urgent it seems to ration access to jobs and to impede useful unemployment that would threaten the volume of the labour market. The inverse, of course, is equally possible: a modern society in which frustrated workers organize to protect the freedom of people to be useful outside the activities that result in the production of commodities. But again, this social alternative depends on a new, rational, and cynical competence of the common man when faced with the professional imputation of needs.

[5]

OUTFLANKING
THE NEW PROFESSIONAL

Today, professional power is clearly threatened by increasing evidence of the counterproductivity of its output. People are beginning to see that such hegemony deprives them of their right to politics. The symbolic power of experts which, while defining needs, eviscerates personal competence is now seen to be more perilous than their technical capability, which is confined to servicing the needs they create. Simultaneously, one hears the repeated call for the enactment of legislation that might lead us beyond an age dominated by the professional ethos: the demand that professional and bureaucratic licensing be replaced by the investiture of elected citizens, rather than altered by the inclusion of consumer representatives on licensing boards; the demand that prescription rules in pharmacies, curricula, and other pretentious supermarkets be relaxed; the demand for the protection of *productive* liberties; the demand for the right to practice without a license; the demand for public utilities that facilitate client evaluation of all practitioners who work for money. In response to these threats, the major professional establishments, each in its own way, use three fundamental strategies to shore up the erosion of their legitimacy and power.

The self-critical hooker

The first approach is represented by the Club of Rome. Fiat, Volkswagen, and Ford pay economists, ecologists, and experts in social control to identify the products industries ought not to produce, in order to strengthen the industrial system. Also, doctors in the Club of Kos now recommend that surgery, radiation, and chemotherapy be abandoned in the treatment of most cancers, since these treatments usually prolong and intensify suffering without adding to the life of the treated. Lawyers and dentists promise to police, as never before, the competence, decency, and rates of their fellow professionals.

A variant of this approach is seen in some individuals or their organizations, who challenge the American Bar Association, British Medical Association, and other power brokers of the establishment. These claim to be radical because, 1) they advise consumers against the interests of the majority of their peers; 2) they tutor laymen on how to behave on hospital, university, or police governing boards; and 3) they occasionally testify to legislative committees on the uselessness of procedures proposed by the professions and demanded by the public. For example, in a province of Western Canada doctors prepared a report on some two dozen medical procedures for which the legislature was considering a budget increase. All the procedures were costly, and the doctors pointed out that they were also very painful, and many were dangerous, and that none could be proven effective. For the time being the legislators refused to act on such medical advice, a failure that, provisionally, tends to reinforce the belief in the necessity of *professional* protection against professional hubris.

Professional self-policing is useful principally in catching the grossly incompetent – the butcher or the outright charlatan. But as has been shown again and again, it only protects the inept and cements the dependence of the public on their services. The 'critical' doctor, the 'radical' lawyer, or the 'advocacy' architect seduces clients away from his colleagues, who are less aware than he of the vagaries of fashion. First liberal professions sell the public on the need for their services by promising to watch over the poorer layman's schooling, ethics or inservice training. Then dominant professions insist on their rightful duty to guide and further disable the public by organizing into clubs that brandish the high consciousness of

88

ecological, economic, and social constraints. Such action inhibits the further extension of the professional sector but strengthens public dependence within that sector. The idea that professionals have a *right* to serve the public is thus of very recent origin. Their struggle to establish and legitimate this corporate right becomes one of our most oppressive social threats.

The alliance of hawkers

The second strategy seeks to organize and coordinate professional response in a manner that purportedly is more faithful to the multifaceted character of human problems. Also, this approach seeks to utilize ideas borrowed from systems analysis and operations research in order to provide more national and all-encompassing solutions. An example of what this means in practice can be taken from Canada. Some years ago, the Minister of Health launched a campaign to convince the public that spending more money on physicians would not change the country's patterns of disease and death. He pointed out that premature loss of life-time was due overwhelmingly to three factors: accidents, mostly in motor vehicles; heart disease and lung cancer, which doctors are notoriously powerless to heal; and suicide combined with murder, phenomena that are outside medical control. The minister called for new approaches to health and for the retrenchment of medicine. The task of protecting, restoring, or consoling those made sick by the destructive life-style and environment typical of contemporary Canada was taken up by a great variety of new and old professions. Architects discovered that they had a mission to improve Canadians' health; dog-control was found to be an inter-departmental problem calling for new specialists. A new corporate biocracy intensified control over the organisms of Canadians with a thoroughness the old iatrocracy could hardly have imagined. The slogan 'better spend money in order to stay healthy than on doctors when you get sick' can now be recognized as the hawking of new hookers who want the money spent on them.

The practice of medicine in the United States illustrates a similar dynamic. There, a coordinated approach to the health of Americans has become enormously expensive without being especially effective. In 1950, the typical wage-earner transferred less than two weeks pay per year to professional health care. In 1976, the proportion was up to around five to seven weeks pay per year: buying a new Ford, one now pays more for worker hygiene than for the metal the car contains. Yet with all this effort and expense, the life expectancy of the *adult* male population has not sensibly changed in the last one hundred years. It is lower than in many poor countries, and has been declining slowly but steadily for the last twenty years.

Where disease patterns have changed for the better, it has been due principally to the adoption of a healthier life-style, especially in diet. To a small degree, inoculations and the routine administration of such simple interventions as antibiotics, contraceptives, or Carman tubes have contributed to the decline of certain diseases. But such procedures do not postulate the need for professional services. People cannot become healthier by being more firmly wedded to a medical profession, yet many 'radical' doctors call for just such an increased biocracy. They seem to be unaware that a more rational 'problem-solving' approach is simply another version, though perhaps more sophisticated, of affirmative action.

The professionalization of the client

The third strategy to make dominant professions survive is this year's radical chic. As the prophets of the sixties drooled about development on the door-steps of affluence these myth makers mouth about the self-help of professionalized clients.

In the United States alone since 1965, about 2700 books have appeared that teach you how to be your own patient, so that you need see the doctor only when it is worthwhile for him. Some books recommend that only after due training and examination should graduates in self-medication be empowered to buy aspirin and dispense it to their children. Others suggest that professionalized patients should receive preferential rates in hospitals and that they should benefit from lower insurance premiums. Only women with a license to practice home birth should have their children outside hospitals since such professional mothers can, if necessary, be sued for malpractice. I have seen a 'radical' proposal that such a license to birth be obtained under feminist rather than medical auspices.

The professional dream of rooting each hierarchy of needs in the grassroots goes under the banner of self-help. At present it is promoted by the new tribe of experts in self-help who have replaced the experts in development of the sixties. The universal professionalization of clients is their aim. American building experts who last autumn invaded Mexico serve as an example of the new Crusade. About two years ago a Boston professor of architecture came to Mexico for a vacation. A Mexican friend of mine took him beyond the airport where, during the last twelve years, a new city had grown up. From a few huts, it had mushroomed into a community three times the size of Cambridge, Massachusetts. My friend, also an architect, wanted to show him the thousands of examples of peasant ingenuity with patterns, structures, and uses of refuse not in and therefore not derivable from textbooks. He should not have been surprised that his colleague took several hundred rolls of pictures of these brilliant amateur inventions that make the two-million-person slum work. The pictures were analyzed in Cambridge; and by the end of the year, new-baked United States specialists in community architecture were busy teaching the people of Ciudad Netzahualcoyotl their problems, needs, and solutions.

[6]

THE POST-PROFESSIONAL
ETHOS

The inverse of professionally certified lack, need, and poverty is modern subsistence. The term 'subsistence economy' is now generally used only to designate group survival which is marginal to market-dependence and in which people make what they use by means of traditional tools and within an inherited, often unexamined, social organization. I propose to recover the term by speaking about modern subsistence. Let us call modern subsistence the style of life that prevails in a post-industrial economy in which people have succeeded in reducing their market

93

dependence, and have done so by protecting – by political means – a social infrastructure in which techniques and tools are used primarily to generate use-values that are unmeasured and unmeasurable by professional need-makers. I have developed a theory of such tools elsewhere (*Tools for Conviviality*, Calder & Boyars, 1973), proposed the technical term 'convivial tool' for use-value-orientated engineered artefacts. I have shown that the inverse of progressive modernized poverty is politically generated convivial austerity that protects freedom and equity in the use of such tools.

A retooling of contemporary society with convivial rather than industrial tools implies a shift of emphasis in our struggle for social justice; it implies a new kind of subordination of distributive to participatory justice. In an industrial society, individuals are trained for extreme specialization. They are rendered impotent to shape or to satisfy their own needs. They depend on commodities and on the managers who sign the prescriptions for them. The right to diagnosis of need, prescription of therapy, and – in general – distribution of goods predominates in ethics, politics, and law. This emphasis on the right to imputed necessities shrinks the liberty to learn or to heal or to move on one's own to fragile luxuries. In a convivial society, the opposite would be true. The protection of equity in the exercise of personal liberties would be the predominant concern of a society based on radical technology: science and technique at the service of a more effective use-value generation. Obviously, such equitably distributed liberty would be meaningless if it were not grounded in the right of equal access to raw materials, tools, and utilities. Food, fuel, fresh air, or living space can no more be equitably distributed than wrenches or jobs unless they are rationed without regard to imputed need, that is, in equal *maximum* amounts to young and old, cripple and president. A society dedicated to the protection of equally distributed, modern and effective tools for the exercise of productive liberties cannot come into existence unless the commodities and resources on which the exercise of these liberties is based are equally distributed to all.